Data Science 101

The Ultimate Guide on What you Need to Know to Work with Data Using Python, Tips, and Tricks to Learn Data Analytics, Machine Learning, and Their Application

Andrew Park

Data Science 101

Table of Contents

INTRODUCTION 8

CHAPTER 1: DATA SCIENCE ALGORITHMS AND MODELS . 10

NEURAL NETWORKS 10

NAÏVE BAYES 14

CLUSTERING ALGORITHMS 15

SUPPORT VECTOR MACHINES 17

DECISION TREES 19

K-NEAREST NEIGHBORS 20

THE MARKOV ALGORITHM 22

CHAPTER 2: REGRESSION ANALYSIS (LINEAR AND
LOGISTIC REGRESSION) 24

LINEAR REGRESSION 25

Linear Regression in Python 27

LOGISTIC REGRESSION 30

Applications of Logistic Regression 34

LOGISTIC REGRESSION VS. LINEAR REGRESSION 37

Advantages of logistic regression 37

HOW DOES MACHINE LEARNING COMPARE TO AI 38

What is Artificial Intelligence? 39

How is Machine Learning different? 40

CHAPTER 3: DATA AGGREGATION AND GROUP
OPERATIONS 44

WHAT IS DATA AGGREGATION 46

CHAPTER 4: PRACTICAL CODES AND EXERCISES TO USE
PYTHON 50

Creating a Magic 8 Ball 50

How to make a Hangman Game 52

Making your own K-means algorithm 55

CHAPTER 5: FUNCTIONS AND MODULES IN PYTHON 62

THE SYNTAX OF FUNCTIONS 62

HOW FUNCTIONS ARE CALLED IN PYTHON 63

Docstring *64*

The return statement *65*

CHAPTER 6: INTERACTION WITH DATABASES 66

THE PICKLE MODULE 66

THE SQLITE3 MODULE 68

The SQLObject Package *71*

BUILDING A DIGITAL SPIDER *71*

Specifying the Database *72*

Specifying the database ideatable. *73*

CHAPTER 7: DATA MINING TECHNIQUES IN DATA SCIENCE
.... *76*

MAPREDUCE TECHNIQUE 76

DISTANCE MEASURES *77*

LINK ANALYSIS 78

PAGERANK 78

THE CONTENT 79

DATA STREAMING 79

SAMPLING DATA IN A STREAM 80

FILTERING STREAMS 80

COUNT SPECIFIC ELEMENTS IN A STREAM 81

FREQUENT ITEM – SET ANALYSIS 81

CHAPTER 8: DATA IN THE CLOUD 84

WHAT IS THE CLOUD? 84

Network *85*

Data Science in the Cloud *86*

Software Architecture and Quality Attributes *88*

Sharing Big Data in the Cloud *88*

CLOUD AND BIG DATA GOVERNANCE 89

Need for Data Cloud Tools to Deliver High Value of Data............90

CONCLUSION **92**

Introduction

Python is one of the top programming languages, universities and industries are preferring to teach it and use respectively. The charm of Python is hidden in the fact that it has extremely large applications in a wide range of fields. Most people abhor Python because of its use in building artificial intelligence models. They fear that these Python-powered AI models will drive people out of different industries and snatch their jobs. They quote the example of Tesla's driverless taxi program by which Tesla pretends to replace Uber's taxis in the US market. But the reality is different. In fact, Python-powered AI models will create many more jobs instead of removing jobs For example, building these models will become an independent industry. Also, the implementation of these AI models will become a new business sector.

Data science is going to take the corporate world by storm. Data science is based on Python programming language, as more and more companies are now moving in a neck-on-neck competition. All they crave is a way to take an edge over their competitors. They do each thing for power and to get ahead. In this regard, Python seems to be promising. Python-backed data science tends to equip industries with sophisticated data about past and present sales patterns, which can help corporate sector CEOs make wiser decisions about sales and development of marketing strategies.

The biggest advantage for learners of Python is that you don't have to compile the code. In C++, you have to compile the entire program first and then run it. Only then you will be able to see whether your program runs or returns an error. Python offers the same level of programming and even at a higher stage, but still, it is an interpreted language that can be easily written, edited, and corrected.

Python is very easy to read and learn. You can easily read source codes for different programs that are created by other programmers. But no matter how easy it is on the outside to read and learn, it needs, like all the other programming languages, dedicated practice. You will have to get to the Python editor and practice all codes. In the beginning, you can take the code and just paste it in the editor to see the results. In the second phase, you can make minor edits to the code and see the results. In the third phase, you will be able to completely reshape a program and see how it runs in the Python shell. Given the increasing applications of Python, learning it is extremely profitable from the angle of the global job market. Python can give you the much-needed edge over others when it comes to securing high paid jobs.

Chapter 1: Data Science Algorithms and Models

This guidebook has taken some time to look through a lot of the different parts that come with data analysis. We took a look at what data analysis is all about, how to work with the Python language and why it is such a good thing for the data analysis, and even some of the basics of Machine Learning and why this should be a part of our process.

With all of this in mind, it is now time for us to move on to some of the other things that we can do when working on this process. We are going to explore some of the best algorithms and models that we can use to complete our data analysis with the help of the Python language. There are so many different algorithms that we can choose from, and all of them are going to be great options to get the work done. With this in mind, let's dive right in and see what some of the best algorithms and models are for completing your business data analysis with Python.

Neural Networks

It is hard to have a discussion about Machine Learning and data analysis without taking some time to talk about neural networks and how these forms of coding are meant to work.

Neural networks are a great addition to any Machine Learning model because they can work similarly to the human brain. When they get the answer right, they can learn from that, and some of the synapses that bring it all together will get stronger. The more times that this algorithm can get an answer right, the faster and more efficient it can become with its job as well.

With neural networks, each of the layers that you go through will spend a bit of time at that location, seeing if there is any pattern. This is often done with images or videos so it will go through each layer of that image and see whether or not it can find a new pattern. If the network does find one of these patterns, then it is going to instigate the process that it needs to move over to the following layer. This is a process that continues, with the neural network going through many layers until the algorithm has created a good idea of what the image is and can give an accurate prediction.

There are then going to be a few different parts that can show up when we reach this point, and it depends on how the program is set up to work. If the algorithm was able to go through the process above and could sort through all of the different layers, then it is going to make a prediction. If the prediction it provides is right, the neurons in the system will turn out stronger than ever. This is because the program is going to work with artificial intelligence to make the stronger connections and associations that we need to keep this process going. The more times that our neural network can come back with the correct answer, the more efficient this neural network will become in the future when we use it.

If the program has been set up properly, it is going to make the right prediction that there is a car in the picture. The program can come up with this prediction based on some of the features that it already knows belongs to the car, including the color, the number on the license plate, the placement of the doors, the headlights, and more.

When you are working with some of the available conventional coding methods, this process can be really difficult to do. You will find that the neural network system can make this a really easy system to work with.

For the algorithm to work, you would need to provide the system with an image of the car. The neural network would then be able to look over the picture. It would start with the first layer, which would be the outside edges of the car. Then it would go through some other layers that help the neural network understand if any unique characteristics are present in the picture that outlines that it is a car. If the program is good at doing the job, it is going to get better at finding some of the smallest details of the car, including things like its windows and even wheel patterns.

There could potentially be a lot of different layers that come with this one, but the more layers and details that the neural network can find, the more accurately it will be able to predict what kind of car is in front of it. If your neural network is accurate in identifying the car model, it is going to learn from this lesson. It will remember some of these patterns and characteristics that showed up in the car model and will store them for use later. The next time that they encounter the same kind of car model, they will be able to make a prediction pretty quickly.

When working with this algorithm, you are often going to choose one and use it, when you want to go through a large number of pictures and find some of the defining features that are inside of them. For example, there is often a big use for this kind of thing when you are working with face recognition software. All of the information wouldn't be available ahead of time with this method. And you can teach the computer how to recognize the right faces using this method instead. It is also one that is highly effective when you want it to recognize different animals, define the car models, and more.

As you can imagine, there are several advantages that we can see when we work with this kind of algorithm. One of these is that we can work with this method, and we won't have to worry as much about the statistics that come with it. Even if you need to work with the algorithm and you don't know the statistics or don't have them available, the neural network can be a great option to work with to ensure that any complex relationship will show up.

Naïve Bayes

We can also work with an algorithm that is known as the Naïve Bayes algorithm. This is a great algorithm to use any time that you have people who want to see some more of the information that you are working on, and who would like to get more involved in the process, but they are uncertain about how to do this, and may not understand the full extent of what you are doing. It is also helpful if they want to see these results before the algorithm is all the way done.

As you work through some of the other algorithms on this page and see what options are available for handling the data, you will notice that they often take on hundreds of thousands of points of data. This is why it takes some time to train and test the data, and it can be frustrating for those on the outside to find out they need to wait before they can learn anything about the process. Showing information to the people who make the decisions and the key shareholders can be a challenge when you are just getting started with the whole process.

This is where the Naïve Bayes algorithm comes in. It is able to simplify some of the work that you are doing. It will usually not be the final algorithm that you use, but it can often give a good idea to others outside of the process about what you are doing. It can answer questions, puts the work that you are doing in a much easier to understand the form, and can make sure that everyone will be on the same page.

Clustering algorithms

One of the best types of algorithms that you can work with is going to be the clustering algorithm. There are a variety of clustering algorithms out there to focus on, but they are going to help us ensure that the program can learn something on its own, and will be able to handle separating the different data points that we have. These clustering algorithms work best when you can keep things simple. It takes some of the data that you are working with and then makes some clusters that come together. Before we start with the program, though, we can choose the number of clusters that we want to fit the information too.

The number of clusters that you go with is going to depend on what kind of information you are working with as well. If you just want to separate your customers by gender, then you can work with just two clusters. If you would like to separate the customers by their age or some other feature, then you may need some more clusters to get this done. You can choose the number of clusters that you would like to work with.

The nice thing that comes with the clustering algorithms is that they will handle most of the work of separating and understanding the data for you. This is because the algorithm is in charge of how many points of data go into each of the clusters you choose, whether there are two clusters or twenty that you want to work with. When you take a look at one of these clusters, you will notice that with all of the points inside, it is safe to assume that these data points are similar or share something important. This is why they fell into the same cluster with one another.

Once we can form some of these original clusters, it is possible to take each of the individual ones and divide them up to get some more sets of clusters because this can sometimes provide us with more insights. We can do this a few times, which helps to create more division as we go through the steps. In fact, it is possible to go through these iterations enough times that the centroids will no longer change. This is a sign that it is time to be done with the process.

Support Vector Machines

Another option that we need to work with is known as the support vector machine or SVM. When we work with this one, it is important to take all of the items in our data set, and then work on plotting them into one n-dimensional space, rather than having them all over the place. N is going to be the number of features that should show up in this algorithm along with the rest of our information. We then have the option to take the value of all these features and translate them over to the value that is in your coordinates. From here, we determine where the hyperplane is because this will show us the differences that are there between our various classes.

You may notice while working on this kind of algorithm that more than one support vector is going to show up. Many of these are easy to ignore because they are just the coordinates of individual observations that are seen. You can then use the SVM as a frontier that can separate them into classes. The two support vectors that we need to focus on will be the hyperplane and the line.

To do this, we need to make sure that we know where the hyperplane is. As we go through this process, there can sometimes be more than one hyperplane to pick from depending on the kind of data we are working with. There can also be an additional challenge because we want to ensure that with these options, we go with the one that helps us to understand the data, not one that leads us astray. The good thing to consider here is that even if you do see more than one option to work with, there are a few steps that you can follow to make it easier to pick the right one. The steps that you can follow to make this happen will include:

- We are going to start with three hyperplanes that we will call 1, 2, and 3. Then we are going to spend time figuring out which hyperplane is right so that we can classify the star and the circle.

- The good news is there is a pretty simple rule that you can follow so that it becomes easier to identify which hyperplane is the right one. The hyperplane that you want to go with will be the one that segregates your classes the best.

- That one was easy to work with, but in the next one, our hyperplanes of 1, 2, and 3 are all going through the classes and they similarly segregate them. For example, all of the lines or these hyperplanes are going to run parallel with each other. From here, you may find that it is hard to pick which hyperplane is the right one.

- For the above issue, we will need to use what is known as the margin. This is the distance that occurs between the hyperplane and the nearest data point from either of the two classes. Then you will be able to get some numbers that can help you out. These numbers may be closer together, but they will point out which hyperplane is going to be the best.

With the example that we have above, we see one of the times that this is a great tool to work within Machine Learning. When we look through some of the points of data that are available, and if you notice that there is a pretty good margin that separates some of the points, then this is a good place to work with the SVM model. It is effective and it can help us find some of the results that we want in the process as well.

Decision Trees

Decisions trees are also a good option that we can work with when we want to take a few available options, and then compare them to see what the possible outcome of each option is all about. We can even combine a few of these decision trees to make a random forest and get more results and predictions from this.

The decision tree is going to be one of the best ways to compare a lot of options, and then choose the path that is going to be the best for your needs. Sometimes there are a whole host of options that we can choose from, and many times they will all seem like great ideas. For businesses who need to choose from the best option out of the group, and need to know which one is likely to give them the results that they are looking for, the decision tree is the best option.

With the decision tree, we can place the data we have into it, and then see the likely outcome that is going to result from making a certain decision. This prediction can help us to make smart business decisions based on what we see. If we had a few different options with this and compare the likely outcomes from each one, it is much easier to determine which course of action is the best one for us to take.

K-Nearest Neighbors

The next algorithm that we can look at is known as the K-Nearest Neighbors algorithm or KNN. When we work with this algorithm, the goal is to search through all of the data that we have for the k most similar example of any instance that we want to work with. Once we can complete this process, then the algorithm can move on to the next step, which is where it will look through all of the information that you have and provide you with a summary. Then the algorithm will take those results and give you some of the predictions you need to make good business decisions.

With this learning algorithm, you will notice that the learning you are working with becomes more competitive. This works to your advantage because there will be a big competition going on between the different elements or the different parts in the models so that you can get the best solution or prediction based on the data you have at hand.

There are several benefits that we can receive when it comes to working with this algorithm. For example, it is a great one that cuts through all of that noise that sometimes shows up in our data. This noise, depending on the set of data that you use, can be really loud, and cutting this down a bit, can help make a big difference in the insights that you can see.

And if you are trying to handle and then go through some of the larger amounts of data that some companies have all at once, then this is a great algorithm to go with as well. Unlike some of the others that need to limit the set of data by a bit, the KNN algorithm is going to be able to handle all of your data, no matter how big the set is. Keep in mind that sometimes the computational costs are going to be higher with this kind of method, but in some cases, this is not such a big deal to work with.

To make the K-Nearest neighbors algorithm work the way that you want, there are going to be a few steps that will make this process a little bit easier.

Working with this algorithm can help us to get a lot done

when it is time to work with putting parts together, and seeing where all of our data is meant to lie. If you follow the steps that we have above, you will be able to complete this model for yourself, and see some of the great results in the process when it is time to make predictions and good business decisions.

The Markov Algorithm

Another type of unsupervised Machine Learning algorithm that you can work with is the Markov algorithm. This particular algorithm is going to take the data that you decide to input into it, and then it will translate it to help work in another coding language if you choose. The nice thing here is that you can pick out which rules you want to use with this algorithm ahead of time so that the algorithm will work the way that you want. Many programmers in Machine Learning find that this algorithm, and the fact they can set up their own rules ahead of time, is nice because it allows you to take a string of data and ensure that it is as useful as possible as you learn on the job and figure out the parameters of how the data will behave.

Another thing that you may like about this Markov algorithm is that you can work with it in several ways, rather than being stuck with just one method. One option to consider here is that this algorithm works well with things like DNA. For example, you could take the DNA sequence of someone, and then use this algorithm to translate the information that is inside that sequence into some numerical values. This can often make it easier for programmers, doctors, and scientists and more to know what information is present, and to make better predictions into the future. When you are working with programmers and computers, you will find that the numerical data is going to be much easier to sort through than other options of looking through DNA.

A good reason why you would need to use the Markov algorithm is that it is great at learning problems when you already know the input you want to use, but you are not sure about the parameters. This algorithm is going to be able to find insights that are inside of the information. In some cases, these insights are hidden and this makes it hard for the other algorithms we have discussed to find them.

There are still some downfalls to working with the Markov algorithm. This one can sometimes be difficult to work with because you do need to manually go through and create a new rule any time that you want to bring in a new programming language. If you only want to work with one type of programming language on your project, then this is not going to be a big deal. But many times, your program will need to work with several different languages, and going in and making the new rules a bunch of times can get tedious.

Chapter 2: Regression Analysis (Linear and Logistic Regression)

Several industries across the globe are struggling with the best way to come up with the correct data or information that will eventually enable them to solve their incurring prediction problems. Several banks have made some losses, especially within their credit section as they could not correctly predict the trustfulness of the defaulters. In the health sector, you realize many have lost their lives because of poor planning and risk management, which come as a result of the lack of modeling to tool for more straightforward prediction. We also have other sectors such as weather forecasting where farmers were not advised on the occurrence of rain, as a result leading to more losses. Another area involved the payment of mortgage by homeowners. Due to all these, everyone across the universe went on a rampage looking for the best possible way to handle the prediction roles of the organizations. Later on, all these gave birth to what is termed as regression analysis.

Therefore, regression analysis refers to statistical processes for prediction analysis using variables. In that, it helps in identifying the variables relationships. This analysis consists of both independent and dependent variables. In other words, regression analysis aids in understanding the effect of one independent variable on the dependent variable when other independent variables are kept constant. In most cases, regression analysis will try hard to predict the conditional expectation, especially of the dependent variable.

Regression analysis is applied in several areas such as weather forecasting and prediction. Here, it helps predict the outcome of the rain within a specific period. It is also applicable in other fields such as medical sectors for predicting the chances of diseases. Regression analysis comprises of the following: linear regression, logistic regression, polynomial, stepwise, ridge, lasso, and elastic net regression. All in all, this chapter will only tackle the most widely used regression analysis, such as linear regression and logistic regression. It is good to note that ElasticNet regression is a combination of the Lasso and Ridge regression.

Linear Regression

Linear regression refers to a statistical approach used for modeling a relationship between various variables in a particular set of different independent variables. In this chapter, you'll learn more about dependent variables such as response as well as independent variables, including features of simplicity. To be able to offer extensive search results and have a clear understanding of linear regression in Python, you need to be keen on a primary basis. We begin with the primary version of the subject. For instance, what is a simple linear regression?

By definition, simple linear regression refers to a significant approach that's used in predicting a significant response by utilizing a single feature. Therefore, it's assumed that the main two variables, in this case, are directly related. That's why it's vital to determine the linear function since it often predicts the main response value of the equation accurately. There are different regression models utilized in showing as well as predicting the main relationship between two different variables as well as factors. As such, it's important to note that the main factor that's being predicted is known as the dependent variable. But the factors utilized in predicting the main value of the dependent variable is identified as the independent variable. With that said, it's also vital to note that good data doesn't always narrate the entire story as it may be. Therefore, regression analysis is often used in the research as well as the establishment of the correlation of variables. However, correlation isn't the same as the subject of causation. Therefore, a line found in a simple linear regression that may be fitting into the data points appropriately may not indicate a definitive element regarding a major cause and effect relationship. When it comes to linear regression, every observation has two values. Therefore, one of the values is specifically for the dependent variable. The other is certainly for the independent variable.

Linear Regression in Python

When discussing the simple linear regression analysis, we are looking at some of the simplest forms of regression analysis that are used on various independent variables as well as one independent variable.

Consequently, in such a model, a straight line is often used in approximating the main relationship between an independent as well as a dependent variable. Multiple regression analysis occurs when there are 2 major independent variables applied in regression analysis. As a result, the model is not going to be a slightly simple linear one. Usually, this model ($y= \beta 0 + \beta 1 + E.$) represents a simple linear regression.

By applying the relevant mathematical convention, two main factors are herein involved. They include x and y, which are the main designations. Also, the equation often describes how y correlates with x. This is what is defined as the regression model. Apart from that, the linear regression model has an error term which is often represented by E. It can also be termed as the Greek letter epsilon. Usually, this error term is applied to mainly account for the variability found in y. However, this element cannot be explained in terms of the linear relationship found between x as well as y. It's also important to note that parameters are representing the major population being studied. Some of these parameters represent the main population that is being studied. Usually, a regression line can easily show how a unique positive linear relationship, no relationship, as well as a negative relationship.

With that said, if the line that has been graphed appears to be in a simple linear regression that's flat in any way, no relationship will be found in the two variables. On the other hand, if the regression line slopes upwards with the line's lower end located at y, on the graph, then there will be a positive linear relationship within the graph. But if the regression line tends to slope downward where the upper end of y that intercepts at the graph's axis. In the case where the parameters are well identified and known, the equation of the simple linear regression can utilize the computed meaning of the value of y. But in real practice, various parameter values aren't known. Therefore, they have to be estimated using some forms of data sampling from the actual population.

Therefore, the parameters of these populations are often estimated using sample statistics. These statistics can be represented using b0 + b1.

It is clear that we live in a world that requires us to use tons of data coupled with powerful computers as well as artificial intelligence. While this may only be the beginning, there is a rise in the use of Data Science in various sectors across the world. Machine learning is also driving image recognition as well as autonomous vehicles development and decisions based in the sector of finance as well as the energy industry.

As such, linear regression in Python is still a fundamental statistical as well as Machine Learning technique. Therefore, for those who aspire to do statistics or scientific computing, there are high chances that this will be a requirement in the course work. Not only it is advisable to indulge in the learning process but also proceed to various complex methods appended to the studies.

It's important to understand the different types of linear regression. One of them includes multiple linear regressions that involve a unique case of the linear regression that has two to more independent variables. As such, in a case where there are two independent variables, it happens that the probable regression function is going to represent a major regression plane situated in a three-dimensional space. As such, the objective of the regression appears to be the value that will determine different weights. This also happens to be as close to the actual response as possible. In a different scenario, the case that exceeds two independent variables is often similar.

However, it's more general as well. In a similar case, you may regard polynomial regression as a major generalized issue of linear regression in Python. With that said, you can easily assume the polynomial dependence found between the output as well as inputs. In that case, your regression function may also be f which can include other non-linear terms.

Usually, linear regression is the initial Machine Learning algorithm that data scientists encounter in their practice. It's a vital model that everyone in the sector should master. This is because it helps in laying a strong foundation for different Machine Learning algorithms. For starters, it may be utilized in forecasting sales by analyzing sales data for initial months. Also, it may be used in gaining important insight regarding consumer behavior.

Logistic Regression

Logistic regression comprises of logistic model, logistic function, statistics model, and much more. Therefore, many organizations apply logistic regression in their day to day activities which mainly composed of data predictions and analysis. You can always conduct this regression analysis, especially when the dependent variable is binary. That's dichotomous.

Just like other types of regression analyses, logistic regression is entirely applied in any analysis dealing with prediction. Its primary function, in this case, is to describe data. Also, logistic regression can be used to explain or illustrate the kind of relationship between the binary variable, which is the dependent one, and the other variables, which are the independent ones. This regression might look challenging to interpret, but with the help of specific tools such as Intellectus Statistics, you can easily undertake your data analysis.

Logistic regression knowledge can be easily applied in statistics with the help of the logistic model. In this case, the primary function of the logistic model is actually to come up with the correct results of certain predictions or classes with the help of probability. For example, probability works best in areas where you are only required to predict the outcome of the existing events. These events include: healthy or sick, win or lose, alive or dead, or even in places where you are making your analysis about the test where someone either fails or passes. Still, in this model, you will be able to fine-tune your result primarily through probability. In the case of an image, you will be able to extend your model to cover up various classes. You will be able to detect whether the image in your analysis is a lion or a cat, and so on. In this case, the individual variables within the image will have their probability numbers between 0 and 1. However, the sum here should be adding up to one.

Therefore, logistic regression refers to a basic statistical model that makes greater use of the available logistic function regardless of the complexity of more extensions that might exist. Logistic regression is part and parcel of the regression analysis, and on many occasions, it is applied in various analyses where logistic model parameters are estimated. Remember, the logistic model is like a form or a type of binary regression. Therefore, a binary regression consists of a binary logistic model. This model is composed of a dependent variable which includes two possible values of events. These values can be represented as pass/fail, alive/dead, good/bad, and much more. You need to note that the indicator variable actually denotes these possible values and always they have labeled 0 and 1. Within this logistic model, the odds logarithm that's log-odds, for the values of 1 represents a linear combination. In that, this combination has got one or more variables that are entirely independent. In this case, they are called predictors here.

Moreover, in logistic regression analysis, independent

variables sometimes may each form a binary variable or sometimes a continuous variable. In the case of a binary variable, there must be the presence of two classes or events, and they have to be coded by the indicator variables. However, on the other hand, continuous variable represents real value. In the logistic regression analysis, the corresponding probability of these values always varies between 0 and 1 as has been denoted previously above. In this analysis, these log-odds, that's, algorithms of odds will be converted by logistic function into probability. Log odds are measured in logit which also a derivative of its name (logistic unit). Again, you can also use a probit model with a different sigmoid function to convert the log odds into a probability for easy analysis. You need to note that the probit model is an example of an analogous model which comprises of the sigmoid function.

All in all, you will realize that the logistic model is the most preferred in this conversion due to its defining attributes or characteristics. One such feature of the logistic model is its ability to increase the multiplicatively scales of each of the independent variables. As a result of this, it produces an outcome with parameters assigned to each independent variable at a constant rate. However, this will generalize the odd ratio if at all, it is part of a variable which is a binary dependent.

It is also good to note that there are extensions when it comes to dependent variables, especially in some regression such as binary logistic. However, this extension is only applicable where two or more levels are used. These two extensions include multinomial logistic regression which works best with categorical outputs, especially the one having several values that's, two values and above. The next type of logistic regression extension is the ordinal logistic regression which deals with a huge collection of multiple categories. A good example here is the ordinal logistic model dealing with the proportional odds. However, this system only does modeling and not performing any classifications dealing with the statistics since it is not a classifier. Therefore, it will only convert the probability input into an output. Following this, let us discuss the applications of logistic regression in a real-life situation.

Applications of Logistic Regression

Logistic regression is applied in metrological and other forecasting stations which consist of meteorologists. The algorithm here is used to predict the probability of rain. This information is vital as it helps in many sectors such as agricultural, transport and so on. Time of planting can efficiently be planned for, and the right arrangement can be put into place.

This analysis is also applied in some risk management systems such as the credit control system. Here, the analysis will predict whether the account holder is a defaulter when it comes to payment or not. Still, on this, the regression analysis will predict the exact amount that someone can be given by using the previous records. This always enables many organizations to run, as they can control everything when it comes to risk management. All accounts will undergo a critical analysis before any credit is appended. Logistic regression is also applied in political sectors, especially during an election. Here, it gives out the probability of winning and losing each candidate owing to their strengths and resources they used. Again, this regression analysis will be able to predict the number of people who might fail to vote and who will vote at the end and to which particular candidate. Some factors help determine the prediction outcome here such as the age of the candidate, sex, the incomes of both the candidate and the voters, state of the residence of both and the total number of votes in the last elections.

Logistic regression is also applied in various medical fields. It is applied in epidemiology. Here, the analysis is used to identify all those risk factors that may eventually result in diseases. As a result, precautions and other preventive measures may be put into place. Its knowledge is usable in the Trauma and Injury Severity Score(TRISS) where predictions of mortality, especially in injured patients, are done. We have several medical scales that have been designed to check on the severity of patients across the globe.

All these medical scales have been developed or managed using logistic regression. In most cases, especially within the health sector, you can use this knowledge to predict the risk of acquiring some dangerous diseases. For example, diseases such as coronary heart disease, diabetes, and other forms of health-related complications can be easily controlled. These predictions are based on the day to day observable characteristics of the individual patient. The traits or characteristics here include the body mass index, sex, age, and even different results of their blood tests. This will eventually help in proper planning and risk management in the medical sector.

Again, this knowledge can be applied in the engineering sector. Here, it is used to predict the failure probability of a particular system, a new product, or even any kind of process. In the field of marketing, logistic regression analysis helps to determine the buyers' purchasing power, their propensity to purchase, and also this knowledge can be used to stop the various subscriptions of the companies. The technique is also applied in economics. Here, knowledge is used to predict the outcome of being involved in the public labor sector. We also have this technique in the issues to do with the probability of homeowners not paying a mortgage. Natural language processing uses conditional random fields which is also an extension of logistic regression, especially to sequential data.

Logistic Regression vs. Linear Regression

You may be wondering about the main difference between these two examples of regressions. In terms of the outcome, linear regression is responsible for the continuous prediction while there is a discrete outcome in logistic regression. A model predicting the price of a car will depend on various parameters like color, year of make, and so on. Therefore, this value will always be different, indicating the continuous outcome. However, a discrete outcome is always one thing. That's, in case of sickness, you can either be sick or not.

Advantages of logistic regression

- It is very effective and efficient
- You can get an outcome without large computational resources
- You can easily interpret it
- No input features required for the scaling process

- No tuning required
- You can easily regularize logistic regression

How Does Machine Learning Compare to AI

One thing that we need to spend some time working on and understanding before we move on is the difference between Artificial Intelligence and Machine learning. Machine learning is going to do a lot of different tasks when we look at the field of Data Science, and it also fits into the category of artificial intelligence at the same time. But we have to understand that Data Science is a pretty broad term, and there are going to be many concepts that will fit into it. One of these concepts that fit under the umbrella of Data Science is Machine Learning, but we will also see other terms that include big data, data mining, and artificial intelligence. Data science is a newer field that is growing more as people find more uses for computers and use these more often.

Another thing that you can focus on when you bring out Data Science is the field of statistics, and it is going to be put together often in Machine Learning. You can work with the focus on classical statistics, even when you are at the higher levels so that the data set will always stay consistent throughout the whole thing. Of course, the different methods that you use to make this happen will depend on the type of data that is put into this and how complex the information that you are using gets as well.

This brings up the question here about the differences that show up between Machine Learning and artificial intelligence and why they are not the same thing. There are a lot of similarities that come with these two options, but the major differences are what sets them apart, and any programmer who wants to work with Machine Learning has to understand some of the differences that show up. Let's take some time here to explore the different parts of artificial intelligence and Machine Learning so we can see how these are the same and how they are different.

What is Artificial Intelligence?

The first thing we are going to take a look at is artificial intelligence or AI. This is a term that was first brought about by a computer scientist named John McCarthy in the 1950s. AI was first described as a method that you would use for manufactured devices to learn how to copy the capabilities of humans concerning mental tasks.

However, the term has changed a bit in modern times, but you will find that the basic idea is the same. When you implement AI, you are enabling machines, such as computers, to operate and think just like the human brain can. This is a benefit that means that these AI devices are going to be more efficient at completing some tasks than the human brain.

At first glance, this may seem like AI is the same as Machine Learning, but they are not exactly the same. Some people who don't understand how these two terms work can think that they are the same, but the way that you use them in programming is going to make a big difference.

How is Machine Learning different?

Now that we have an idea of what artificial intelligence is all about, it is time to take a look at Machine Learning and how this is the same as artificial intelligence, and how this is different. When we look at Machine Learning, we are going to see that this is a bit newer than a few of the other options that come with Data Science as it is only about 20 years old. Even though it has been around for a few decades so far, it has been in the past few years that our technology and the machines that we have are finally able to catch up to this and Machine Learning is being used more.

Machine learning is unique because it is a part of Data Science that can focus just on having the program learn from the input, as well as the data that the user gives to it. This is useful because the algorithm will be able to take that information and make some good predictions. Let's look at an example of using a search engine. For this to work, you would just need to put in a term to a search query, and then the search engine would be able to look through the information that is there to see what matches up with that and returns some results.

The first few times that you do these search queries, it is likely that the results will have something of interest, but you may have to go down the page a bit to find the information that you want. But as you keep doing this, the computer will take that information and learn from it to provide you with choices that are better in the future. The first time, you may click on like the sixth result, but over time, you may click on the first or second result because the computer has learned what you find valuable.

With traditional programming, this is not something that your computer can do on its own. Each person is going to do searches differently, and there are millions of pages to sort through. Plus, each person who is doing their searches online will have their preferences for what they want to show up. Conventional programming is going to run into issues when you try to do this kind of task because there are just too many variables. Machine learning has the capabilities to make it happen, though.

Of course, this is just one example of how you can use Machine Learning. In fact, Machine Learning can help you do some of these complex problems that you want the computer to solve. Sometimes, you can solve these issues with the human brain, but you will often find that Machine Learning is more efficient and faster than what the human brain can do.

Of course, it is possible to have someone manually go through and do this for you as well, but you can imagine that this would take too much time and be an enormous undertaking. There is too much information, they may have no idea where to even get started when it comes to sorting through it, the information can confuse them, and by the time they get through it all, too much time has passed and the information, as well as the predictions that come out of it, are no longer relevant to the company at all.

Machine Learning changes the game because it can keep up. The algorithms that you can use with it can handle all of the work while getting the results back that you need, in almost real-time. This is one of the big reasons that businesses find that it is one of the best options to go with to help them make good and sound decisions, to help them predict the future, and it is a welcome addition to their business model.

Chapter 3: Data Aggregation and Group Operations

Taking the time to categorize our set of data, and giving a function to each of the different groups that we have, whether it is transformation or aggregation, is often going to be a critical part of the workflow for data analysis. After we take the time to load, merge, and prepare a set of data, it is then time to compute some more information, such as the group statistics or the pivot tables. This is done to help with reporting or with visualizations of that data.

There are a few options that we can work with here to get this process done. But Pandas is one of the best because it provides us with a flexible interface. We can use this interface to slice, dice, and then summarize some of the sets of data we have more easily.

One reason that we see a lot of popularity for SQL and relational databases of all kinds is that we can use them to ease up the process which joins, filters, transforms, and aggregates the data that we have. However, some of the query languages, including SQL, that we want to use are going to be more constrained in the kinds of group operations that we can perform right with them.

As we are going to see with some of the expressiveness that happens with the Pandas library, and with Python, in general, we can perform a lot of more complex operations. This is done by simply utilizing any function that can accept an array from NumPy or an object from Pandas.

Each of the grouping keys that you want to work with can end up taking a variety of forms. And we can see that the keys don't have to all come in as the same type. Some of the forms that these grouping keys can come in for us to work on include:

- An array or a list that is the same length as the axis that we want to group.
- A value that is going to indicate the name of the column in a DataFrame.
- A Series that is going to give the correspondence between the values of the axis that is being grouped here, and the group names you have.
- A function that can then be invoked on the axis index, or on some of the individual labels in the index.

Note that the last three methods of this are going to be a type of shortcut that helps us to produce an array of values to be used when splitting up the object. This can seem a bit abstract right now, but don't let this bother you. It will all make more sense as we go through the steps and learn more about how all of this is meant to work. With this in mind, it is time to talk more about data aggregation and how we can make this work for our needs.

What is Data Aggregation

Data aggregation is any kind of process in which information can be gathered and then expressed in the form of a summary, usually for analysis. One of the common purposes that come with aggregation is to help us get some more information about a particular topic or a group, based on a lot of variables like profession, income, and age.

The information about these groups is often going to be used to personalize a website, allowing them to choose what content and advertising that is likely to appeal to an individual who belongs to one or more groups where the data was originally collected from. Let's take a look at how this works.

We can work with a site that is responsible for selling music CDs. They could use the ideas of data aggregation to advertise specific types of CD's based on the age of the user, and the data aggregate that is collected for others in that age group.

The OLAP, or Online Analytic Processing, is a simple option with data aggregation in which the market is going to use mechanisms for online reporting to help the business process through all of this information.

Data aggregation can be a lot of different things as well. For example, it could be more user-based than some of the other programs that we may have seen in the past. Personal data aggregation services are popular, and they will offer any user a single point for collection of their personal information from a host of other websites that we want to work with.

In these systems, the customer is going to work with a single master PIN, or personal identification number, which allows them the access they need to various accounts. This could include things like music clubs, book clubs, airlines, financial institutions, and so on. Performing this type of data aggregation can take some time and will be a more complex system to put in, but we will see that it comes under the title of screen scraping.

This is just one example of how we can work through the process of data aggregation. It is one of the best methods to help companies to gain the knowledge and the power that they need based on the users they have at the time. It often works well with Pandas, Python, and even databases because it can collect a lot of the information that is found in those, and then recommends options to our customers or our users, based on where they fit in with the rest of the information.

Yes, there are always going to be some outliers to the information, and times when the information is not going to apply to a person no matter where they fit in the database or how good the data aggregation algorithms are. But it will be able to increase the likelihood that you will reach the customers and the users you want, providing them with the information and the content that they need, based on their features and how they will react compared to other similar customers.

Chapter 4: Practical Codes and Exercises to Use Python

Now that we have had some time to learn how to work with the Python code, it is time to take a look at some practical examples of working with this kind of coding language. We will do a few different Python exercises here so that you can have a little bit of fun, and get a better idea of how you would use the different topics that we have talked about in this guidebook to your benefit. There are a lot of neat programs that you can use when you write in Python, but the ones in this chapter will give you a good idea of how to write codes, and how to use the examples that we talked about in this guidebook in real coding. So let's get started!

Creating a Magic 8 Ball

The first project that we are going to take a look at here is how to create your own Magic 8 ball. This will work just like a regular magic 8 ball, but it will be on the computer. You can choose how many answers that you would like to have available to those who are using the program, but we are going to focus on having eight responses show up for the user at a random order, so they get something different each time.

Setting up this code is easier than you think. Take some time to study this code, and then write it out into the compiler. See how many of the different topics we discussed in this guidebook show up in this code as well.

The code that you need to use to create a program that includes your own Magic 8 ball will include:

```
# Import the modules
import sys
import random
ans = True
while ans:
question = raw_input("Ask the magic 8 ball a question:
(press enter to quit)")
answers = random.randint(1,8)
if question == ""
sys.exit()
elif answers ==1:
print("It is certain")
elif answers == 2:
print("Outlook good")
elif answers == 3:
print("You may rely on it")
elif answers == 4:
print("Ask again later")

elif answers == 5:
print("Concentrate and ask again")
elif answers == 6:
```

```
print("Reply hazy, try again.")
elif answers == 7:
print("My reply is no")
elif answers == 8:
print("My sources say no")
```

Remember, in this program, we chose to go with eight options because it is a Magic 8 ball and that makes the most sense. But if you would like to add in some more options, or work on another program that is similar and has more options, then you would just need to keep adding in more of the elif statement to get it done. This is still a good example of how to use the elif statement that we talked about earlier and can give us some good practice on how to use it. You can also experiment a bit with the program to see how well it works and make any changes that you think are necessary to help you get the best results.

How to make a Hangman Game

The next project that we are going to take a look at is creating your own Hangman game. This is a great game to create because it has a lot of the different options that we have talked about throughout this guidebook and can be a great way to get some practice on the various topics that we have looked at. We are going to see things like a loop present, some comments, and more and this is a good way to work with some of the conditional statements that show up as well.

Now, you may be looking at this topic and thinking it is going to be hard to work with a Hangman game. It is going to have a lot of parts that go together as the person makes a guess and the program tries to figure out what is going on, whether the guesses are right, and how many chances the user gets to make these guesses. But using a lot of the different parts that we have already talked about in this guidebook can help us to write out this code without any problems. The code that you need to use to create your very own Hangman game in Python includes:

```python
# importing the time module
importing time
#welcoming the user
Name = raw_input("What is your name?")
print("Hello, + name, "Time to play hangman!")
print("
"
#wait for 1 second
time.sleep(1)
print("Start guessing...")
time.sleep(.05)
#here we set the secret
word = "secret"
#creates a variable with an empty value
guesses = ' '
#determine the number of turns
turns = 10
#create a while loop
```

```
#check if the turns are more than zero
while turns > 0:
#make a counter that starts with zero
failed = 0
#for every character in secret_word
for car in word:
#see if the character is in the players guess
if char in guesses:

#print then out the character
print char,
else
# if not found, print a dash
print "_",

# and increase the failed counter with one
failed += 1
#if failed is equal to zero
#print You Won
if failed == 0:
print("You Won")
#exit the script
Break
print
# ask the user to guess a character
guess = raw_input("guess a character:")
#set the players guess to guesses
guesses += guess
# if the guess is not found in the secret word
if guess not in word:
```

```
#turns counter decreases with 1 (now 9)
turns -= 1
#print wrong
print("Wrong")
# how many turns are left
Print("You have," + turns, 'more guesses')
#if the turns are equal to zero
if turns == 0
#print "You Lose"
```

Okay, so yes, this is a longer piece of code, especially when it is compared to the Magic 8 Ball that we did above, but take a deep breath, and go through it all to see what you recognize is there. This isn't as bad as it looks, and much of it is comments to help us see what is going on at some of the different parts of the code. This makes it easier to use for our own needs and can ensure that we know what is going on in the different parts. There are probably a lot of other things that show up in this code that you can look over and recognize that we talked about earlier as well. This makes it easier for you to get the code done!

Making your own K-means algorithm

Now that we have had some time to look at a few fun games and examples that you can do with the help of the Python code, let's take a moment to look at some of the things that you can do with Machine Learning and artificial intelligence with your coding. We spent some time talking about how you can work with these and some of the different parts of the code, as well as how Python is going to work with the idea of Machine Learning. And now we are going to take that information and create one of our Machine Learning algorithms to work with as well.

Before we work on a code for this one, we need to take a look at what this k-means clustering means. This is a basic algorithm that works well with Machine Learning and is going to help you to gather up all of the data that you have in your system, the data that isn't labeled at the time, and then puts them all together in their little group of a cluster.

The idea of working with this kind of cluster is that the objects that fall within the same cluster, whether there are just two or more, are going to be related to each other in some manner or another, and they are not going to be that similar to the data points that fall into the other clusters. The similarity here is going to be the metric that you will want to use to show us the strength that is in the relationship between the two.

When you work on this particular algorithm, it is going to be able to form some of the clusters that you need of the data, based on how similar the values of data that you have. You will need to go through and give them a specific value for K, which will be how many clusters that you would like to use. It is best to have at least two, but the number of these clusters that you work with will depend on how much data you have and how many will fit in with the type of data that you are working with.

With this information in mind and a good background of what the K-means algorithm is going to be used for, it is time to explore a bit more about how to write your own codes and do an example that works with K-means. This helps us to practice a bit with Machine Learning and gives us a chance to practice some of our own new Python skills.

```python
import numpy as np
import matplotlib.pyplot as plt
def d(u, v):
    diff = u - v
    return diff.dot(diff)
def cost(X, R, M):
    cost = 0
    for k in xrange(len(M)):
        for n in xrange(len(X)):
            cost += R[n,k]*d(M[k], X[n])
    return cost
```

After this part, we are going to take the time to define your function so that it is able to run the k-means algorithm before plotting the result. This is going to end up with a scatterplot where the color will represent how much of the membership is inside of a particular cluster.

We would do that with the following code:

```
def plot_k_means(X, K, max_iter=20, beta=1.0):
    N, D = X.shape
    M = np.zeros((K, D))
    R = np.ones((N, K)) / K
    # initialize M to random
    for k in xrange(K):
        M[k] = X[np.random.choice(N)]
    grid_width = 5
    grid_height = max_iter / grid_width
    random_colors = np.random.random((K, 3))
    plt.figure()
    costs = np.zeros(max_iter)
    for i in xrange(max_iter):
        # moved the plot inside the for loop
        colors = R.dot(random_colors)
        plt.subplot(grid_width, grid_height, i+1)
        plt.scatter(X[:,0], X[:,1], c=colors)
        # step 1: determine assignments /
responsibilities
        # is this inefficient?
        for k in xrange(K):
            for n in xrange(N):
                R[n,k] = np.exp(-beta*d(M[k], X[n])) /
np.sum( np.exp(-beta*d(M[j], X[n])) for j in xrange(K)
)
        # step 2: recalculate means
```

```
for k in xrange(K):
    M[k] = R[:,k].dot(X) / R[:,k].sum()
costs[i] = cost(X, R, M)
if i > 0:
    if np.abs(costs[i] - costs[i-1]) < 10e-5:
        break
plt.show()
```

Notice here that both the M and the R are going to be matrices. The R is going to become the matrix because it holds onto 2 indices, the k and the n. M is also a matrix because it is going to contain the K individual D-dimensional vectors. The beta variable is going to control how fuzzy or spread out the cluster memberships are and will be known as the hyperparameter. From here, we are going to create a main function that will create random clusters and then call up the functions that we have already defined above.

```
def main():
    # assume 3 means
    D = 2 # so we can visualize it more easily
    s = 4 # separation so we can control how far apart
the means are
    mu1 = np.array([0, 0])
    mu2 = np.array([s, s])
    mu3 = np.array([0, s])
    N = 900 # number of samples
    X = np.zeros((N, D))
    X[:300, :] = np.random.randn(300, D) + mu1
```

```
X[300:600, :] = np.random.randn(300, D) + mu2
X[600:, :] = np.random.randn(300, D) + mu3
# what does it look like without clustering?
plt.scatter(X[:,0], X[:,1])
plt.show()
K = 3 # luckily, we already know this
plot_k_means(X, K)
# K = 5 # what happens if we choose a "bad" K?
# plot_k_means(X, K, max_iter=30)
# K = 5 # what happens if we change beta?
# plot_k_means(X, K, max_iter=30, beta=0.3)
if __name__ == '__main__':
    main()
```

Yes, this process is going to take some time to write out here, and it is not always an easy process when it comes to working through the different parts that come with Machine Learning and how it can affect your code. But when you are done, you will be able to import some of the data that your company has been collecting, and then determine how this compares using the K-means algorithm as well.

Chapter 5: Functions and Modules in Python

In Python programming, functions refer to any group of related statements that perform a given activity. Functions are used in breaking down programs into smaller and modular bits. In that sense, functions are the key factors that make programs easier to manage and organize as they grow bigger over time. Functions are also helpful in avoiding repetition during coding and make codes reusable.

The Syntax of Functions

The syntax of functions refers to the rules which govern the combination of characters that make up a function. These syntaxes include the following:

- The keyword "def" highlights the beginning of every function header.
- A function named is to identify it distinctly. The rules of making functions are the same as the rules which apply for writing identifiers in Python.
- Parameters or arguments via which values are passed onto a function are optional in Python.

- A colon sign (:) is used to highlight the end of every function header.

- The optional documentation string known as "docstring" is used to define the purpose of the function.

- The body of a function is comprised of one or more valid statements in Python. The statements must all have a similar indentation level, (typically four spaces).

- An optional return statement is included for returning a value from a function.

Below is a representation of the essential components of a function as described in the syntax.

```
def function_name(parameters):
''' docstring '''
statement(s)
```

How Functions are Called in Python

Once a function has been defined in Python, it is capable of being called from another function, a program, or the Python prompt even. Calling a function is done by entering a function name with a proper parameter.

Docstring

The docstring is the first string that comes after the function header. The docstring is short for documentation string and is used in explaining what a function does briefly. Although it is an optional part of a function, the documentation process is a good practice in programming. So, unless you have got an excellent memory that can recall what you had for breakfast on your first birthday, you should document your code at all times. In the example shown below, the docstring is used directly beneath the function header.

```
>>> greet("Amos")
Hello, Amos. Good morning!
```

Triple quotation marks are typically used when writing docstrings so they can extend to several lines. Such a string is inputted as the __doc__ attribute of the function. Take the example below.

You can run the following lines of code in a Python shell and see what it outputs:

```
>>> print(greet.__doc__)
This function greets to the person passed into the name
parameter
```

The return statement

The purpose of the return statement is to go back to the location from which it was called after exiting a function.

This statement can hold expressions that have been evaluated and have their values returned. A function will return the Noneobject if the statement is without an expression, or its return statement is itself absent in the function.

For instance:

```
>>> print(greet('Amos'))
Hello, Amos. Good morning!
None
```

In this case, the returned value is None.

Chapter 6: Interaction with Databases

Data management is not a scientific discipline per se. However, increasingly, it permeates the activities of basic scientific work. The increasing volume of data and increasing complexity has long exceeded manageability through simple spreadsheets.

Currently, the need to store quantitative, qualitative data and media of different formats (images, videos, sounds) is very common in an integrated platform from which they can be easily accessed for analysis, visualization or simply consultation.

The Python language has simple solutions to solve this need at its most different levels of sophistication. Following the Python included batteries, its standard library introduces us to the Pickle and cPickle module and, starting with Version 2.5, the SQLite3 relational database.

The Pickle Module

The pickle module and its fastest cPickle cousin implement algorithms that allow you to store Python-implemented objects in a file.

Example of using the pickle module

```
import pickle
class hi:
  def say_hi (self):
    print " hi "
a= hi()
f= open ('pic test','w')
pickle.dump(a, f)
f.close()
f= open ('pic test','r')
b=pickle.load (f)
b.say_hi()
hi
```

As we see in the example of using the pickle module, with the pickle module, we can store objects in a file, and retrieve it without problems for later use. However, an important feature of this module is not evident in example 8.1. When an object is stored using the pickle module, neither the class code nor its data is included, only the instance data.

```
class hi:
  def say_hi (self, name=' alex'):
    print'hi %s !'%name

f= open ('pictest','r')
b=pickle.load (f)
b.say_hi()
hi alex !
```

This way we can modify the class, and the stored instance will recognize the new code as it is restored from the file, as we can see above. This feature means that pickles do not become obsolete when the code they are based on is updated (of course this is only for modifications that do not remove attributes already included in the pickles).

The pickle module is not built for data storage, simply, but for complex computational objects that may contain data themselves. Despite this versatility, it is because it consists of a readable storage structure only by the pickle module itself in a Python program.

The SQLite3 Module

This module becomes part of the standard Python library from Version 2.5. Therefore, it becomes an excellent alternative for users who require the functionality of an SQL1-compliant relational database.

SQLite was born from a C library that had an extremely lightweight database and no concept client-server. In SQLite, the database is a file handled through the SQLite library.

To use SQLite in a Python program, we need to import the SQLite3 module.

```
import sqlite3
```

The next step is the creation of a connection object, through which we can execute SQL commands.

```
c= sqlite 3.connect (' /tmp/ example')
```

We now have an empty database consisting of the example file located in the / tmp directory. SQLite also allows the creation of RAM databases. To do this, simply replace the file name with the string: memory. To insert data into this database, we must first create a table.

```
c.execute (''' create table  specimens (name text, real
height, real weight)''')
< sqlite 3.Cursor object at 0 x83fed10 >
```

Note that SQL commands are sent as strings through the Connection object, execute method. The *create table* command creates a table; it must necessarily be followed by the table name and a list of typed variables (in parentheses), corresponding to the variables contained in this table. This command creates only the table structure. Each specified variable will correspond to one column of the table. Each subsequent entry will form a table row.

```
c.execute (''' insert  into  specimens values (' tom',
1 2.5, 2.3)'''
```

The insert command is another useful SQL command for inserting records into a table.

Although SQL commands are sent as strings over the connection, it is not recommended, for security reasons, to use the string formatting methods ('... values (% s,% s)'% (1,2)) of Python Instead, do the following:

```
t= (' tom',)
c.execute ('select from  specimens where name=?', t)
c.fetch all()
[(' tom', 1 2.5, 2.2 9 9 9 9 9 9 9 9 9 9 9 9 9 9 9 8)]
```

In the example above we use the fetchall method to retrieve the result of the operation. If we wanted to get a single record, we would use fetchone.

Below is how to insert more than one record from existing data structures. In this case, it is a matter of repeating the operation described in the previous example, with a sequence of tubes representing the sequence of records to be inserted.

```
T = ((' j e r r y', 5.1, 0.2), (' butch', 4 2.4, 1
0.3))
for i in t:
   c.execute (' insert into  specimens value s (?, ?,
?)', i)
```

The cursor object can also be used as an iterator to get the result of a query.

```
c.execute (' selectfrom specimens by weight')
```

```
for reg in c:
  print reg
(' jerry', 5.1, 0.2)
(' tom', 1 2.5, 2.2 9 9 9 9 9 9 9 9 9 9 9 9 9 9 9 8)
(' butch', 4 2.4, 1 0.3)
```

The SQLite module is really versatile and useful, but it requires the user to know at least the rudiments of the SQL language. The following solution seeks to solve this problem in a more Pythonic way.

The SQLObject Package

The SQLObject2 package extends the solutions presented so far in two ways: it offers an object-oriented interface to relational databases, and also allows us to interact with multiple databases without having to change our code.

To exemplify sqlobject, we will continue to use SQLite because of its practicality.

Building a Digital Spider

In this example, we will have the opportunity to build a digital spider that will gather information from the web (Wikipedia3) and store it in an SQLite bank via sqlobject.

For this example, we will need some tools that go beyond the database. Let's explore the ability of the standard Python library to interact with the internet, and let's use an external package to decode the pages obtained.

The BeautifulSoup4package is a webpage breaker. One of the most common problems when dealing with Html pages is that many of them have minor design flaws that our browsers ignore, but can hinder further scrutiny.

Hence the value of BeautifulSoup: it is capable of handling faulty pages, returning a data structure with methods that allow quick and simple extraction of the desired information. Also, if the page was created using another encoding, BeautifulSoup, returns all Unicode content automatically without user intervention.

From the standard library, we will use the sys, os, urllib, urllib2 and re modules. The usefulness of each character becomes clear as we move forward in the example.

The first step is to specify the database. SQLObject allows us to choose from MySQL, PostgreSQL, SQLite, Firebird, MAXDB, Sybase, MSSQL, or ADODBAPI. However, as we have already explained, we will restrict ourselves to using the SQLite bank.

Specifying the Database

```
johnsmith= os.path.expanduser (' ~ /. johnsmith' )
```

```
if not os.path.exists (at the dir):
os.mkdir (at the dir)
sqlhub.process Connection = connectionForURI ('
sqlite://'+johnsmithr +'/knowdb')
```

In specifying the database, we create the directory (os.mkdir) where the database will reside (if necessary) and we will natively connect to the database. We use os.path.exists to check if the directory exists. Since we want the directory in the user's folder, and we have no way of knowing beforehand what this directory is, we use os.path.expanduser to replace /home/user as it would normally on the Unix console.

On line 11 of Specifying the database, we see the command that creates the connection to be used by all objects created in this module.

Next, we specify our database table as a class, in which its attributes are the table columns.

Specifying the database ideatable.

```
class Idea (SQLObject): name= UnicodeCol() nlinks=
IntCol()
links= Pickle Col() address = StringCol
```

The class that represents our table is inherited from the SQLObject class. In this class, each attribute (table column) must be assigned an object that gives the type of data to be stored. In this example, we see four distinct types, but there are several others. UnicodeCol represents texts encoded as Unicode, i.e. it can contain characters from any language. IntCol is integer numbers. PickleCol is an exciting type as it allows you to store any type of Python object.

The most interesting thing about this type of column is that it does not require the user to invoke the pickle module to store or read this type of variable. Variables are automatically converted/converted according to the operation. Finally, we have StringCol, which is a simpler version of UnicodeCol, accepting only ASCII character strings. In SQL, it is common to have terms that specify different types according to the length of the text you want to store in a variable. In sqlobject, there is no limit to the size of the text that can be stored in either StringCol or UnicodeCol.

The functionality of our spider has been divided into two classes: Crawler, which is the creeper itself, and the UrlFac class that builds URLs from the word you want in Wikipedia.

Each page is pulled by the urllib2 module. The urlencode function of the urllib module makes it easy to add data to our request so as not to show that it comes from a digital spider. Without this disguise, Wikipedia refuses the connection.

The pages are then parsed by the VerResp method, where

BeautifulSoup has a chance to do its work. Using the SoupStrainer function, we can find the rest of the document, which doesn't interest us, by analyzing only the links (tags 'a') whose destination is URLs beginning with the string/wiki/. All Wikipedia articles start this way. Thus, we avoid chasing external links. From the soup produced, we extract only the URLs, i.e. what comes after "href =".

Chapter 7: Data Mining Techniques in Data Science

The basics of Math and Statistics help a data scientist to build, analyze, and create some complex analytics. To draw accurate insights about the data, data scientists are required to interact with the business side. Business Acumen is a necessity when it comes to analyzing data to help out the business. The results must also be in line with the expectations of the businesses. Therefore, the ability to verbally and visually communicate advanced results and observations to the business and help them easily understand. Data Mining is such a strategy used in Data Science that describes the process where raw data is structured in such a way where one can recognize patterns in the data via mathematical and computational algorithms. Let us an overview of five major data Mining Techniques that every data scientist must be aware of.

Mapreduce Technique

Data Mining applications manage vast amounts of data constantly. You must opt for a new software stack to tackle such applications. Stack software has its file system stored that is called a distributed file system. This file system is used for retrieving parallelism from a computing cluster or clusters. This distributed file system replicates data to enforce security against media failures. Other than this stack file system, there is a higher-level programming system developed to ease the process viz. Mapreduce. Mapreduce is a form of computed implemented in various systems, including Hadoop and Google. Mapreduce implementation is a data mining technique used to tackle large-scale computations. It is easy to implement, i.e.; you have to type only three functions viz. Map and Reduce. The system will automatically control parallel execution and task collaboration.

Distance Measures

The main limitation of data Mining is that it is unable to track similar data/items. Consider an example where you have to track duplicate websites or web content while browsing various websites. Another example can be discovering similar images from a large database. To handle such problems, the Distance Measure technique is made available to you. Distance Measure helps to search for the nearest neighbors in a higher-dimensional space. It is very crucial to define what similarity is. Jaccard Similarity can be one of the examples. The methods used to identify similarity and define the Distance Measure Technique are:

- Shingling
- Min-Hashing
- Locality Sensitive Hashing
- A K-Shingle
- Locality-Sensitive Hashing

Link Analysis

Link Analysis is performed when you can scan the spam vulnerabilities. Earlier, most of the traditional search engines failed to scan the spam vulnerabilities. However, as technology got its wings, Google was able to Introduce some techniques to overcome this problem.

Pagerank

Pagerank techniques use the method of simulation. It monitors every page you are surfing to scan spam vulnerability. This whole process works iteratively, meaning pages that have a higher number of users are ranked better than pages without users visiting.

The Content

The content on every page is determined by some specific phrases used in a page to link with external pages. It is a piece of cake for spammers to modify the internal page where they are administrators, but it becomes difficult for them to modify the external pages. Every page is allocated a real number via a function. The page with a higher rank becomes more important than the page that does not have a considerable page rank. There are no algorithms set for assigning ranks to pages. But for highly confidential or connected Web Graphics, they have a transition matrix based ranking. This principle is used for calculating the rank of a page.

Data Streaming

At times, it is difficult to know datasets in advance; also, the data appears in the form of a stream and gets processed before it disappears. The speed of arrival of the data is so fast that it is difficult to store it in the active storage. Here, data streaming comes into the picture. In the dataStream management system, an unlimited number of streams can be stored in a system. Each data stream produces elements at its own time. Elements have the same rate and time in a particular stream cycle. Such streams are archived into the store. By doing this, it is somewhat difficult to reply to queries already stored in the archival. But such situations are handled by specific retrieval methods. There is a working store as well as an active store that stores the summaries to reply to specific queries. There are certain data Streaming problems viz.

Sampling data in a Stream

You will select attributes to create some samples of the streams. To determine whether all the sample elements belong to the same key sample, you will have to rotate the hashing key of the incoming stream element.

Filtering Streams

To select specific tuples to fit a particular criterion, there is a separate process where the accepted tuples are carried forward, whereas others are terminated and eliminated. There is a modern technique known as Bloon Filtering that will allow you to filter out the foreign elements. The later process is that the selected elements are hashed and collected into buckets to form bits. Bits have a binary working, i.e., 0 and 1. Such bits are set to 1. After this, the elements are set to be tested.

Count Specific Elements in a Stream

If you require to count the unique elements that exist in a universal set, you might have to count each element from the initial step. Flajolet-Martin is a method that often hashes elements to integers, described as binary numbers. By using hash functions and integrating them may result in a reliable estimate.

Frequent Item – Set Analysis

In Frequent Item Set Analysis, we will check the market-basket model and the relationship between them. Every basket contains a set of items, whereas the market will have the data information. The total number of items is always higher than the number of items in the basket. This implies the number of items in the basket can fit in the memory. Baskets are the original and genuine files in the overall distributed system. Each basket is a set of items type. To conclude on the market-basket technique, the characterization of the data depends on this technique to discover frequent itemset. Such sets of items are responsible for revealing most of the baskets. There are many use cases available over the Internet for this technique. This technique was applied previously in some big malls, supermarkets, and chain stores. To illustrate this case, such stores keep track of each of the basket that customer brings to the checkout counter. Here, the items represent the products sold by the store, whereas baskets are a set of items found in a single basket.

Chapter 8: Data in the Cloud

Data Science is a mixture of many concepts. To become a data scientist, it is important to have some programming skills. Even though you might not know all the programming concepts related to infrastructure, but having basic skills in computer science concepts is a must. You must install the two most common and most used programming languages i.e., R and Python, on your computer. With the ever-expanding advanced analytics, Data Science continues to spread its wings in different directions. This requires collaborative solutions like predictive analysis and recommendation systems. Collaboration solutions include research and notebook tools integrated with code source control. Data science is also related to the cloud. The information is also stored in the cloud. So, this lesson will enlighten you with some facts about the "data in the Cloud." So let us understand what cloud means and how the data is stored and how it works.

What is the Cloud?

Cloud can be described as a global server network, each having different unique functions. Understanding networks is required to study the cloud. Networks can be simple or complex clusters of information or data.

Network

As specified earlier, networks can have a simple or small group of computers connected or large groups of computers connected. The largest network can be the Internet. The small groups can be home local networks like Wi-Fi, and Local Area Network that is limited to certain computers or locality. There are shared networks such as media, web pages, app servers, data storage, and printers, and scanners. Networks have nodes, where a computer is referred to as a node. The communication between these computers is established by using protocols. Protocols are the intermediary rules set for a computer. Protocols like HTTP, TCP, and IP are used on a large scale. All the information is stored on the computer, but it becomes difficult to search for information on the computer every time. Such information is usually stored in a data Centre. Data Centre is designed in such a way that it is equipped with support security and protection for the data. Since the cost of computers and storage has decreased substantially, multiple organizations opt to make use of multiple computers that work together that one wants to scale. This differs from other scaling solutions like buying other computing devices. The intent behind this is to keep the work going continuously even if a computer fails; the other will continue the operation. There is a need to scale some cloud applications, as well. Having a broad look at some computing applications like YouTube, Netflix, and Facebook that requires some scaling. We rarely experience such applications failing, as they have set up their systems on the cloud. There is a network cluster in the cloud, where many computers are connected to the same networks and accomplish similar tasks. You can call it as a single source of information or a single computer that manages everything to improve performance, scalability, and availability.

Data Science in the Cloud

The whole process of Data Science takes place in the local machine, i.e., a computer or laptop provided to the data scientist. The computer or laptop has inbuilt programming languages and a few more prerequisites installed. This can include common programming languages and some algorithms. The data scientist later has to install relevant software and development packages as per his/her project. Development packages can be installed using managers such as Anaconda or similar managers. You can opt for installing them manually too. Once you install and enter into the development environment, then your first step, i.e., the workflow starts where your companion is only data. It is not mandatory to carry out the task related to Data Science or Big data on different development machines. Check out the reasons behind this:

1. The processing time required to carry out tasks on the development environment fails due to processing power failure.
2. Presence of large data sets that cannot be contained in the development environment's system memory.
3. Deliverables must be arrayed into a production environment and incorporated as a component in a large application.
4. It is advised to use a machine that is fast and powerful.

Data scientist explores many options when they face such issues; they make use of on-premise machines or virtual machines that run on the cloud. Using virtual machines and auto-scaling clusters has various benefits, such as they can span up and discard it anytime in case it is required. Virtual machines are customized in a way that will fulfill one's computing power and storage needs. Deployment of the information in a production environment to push it in a large data pipeline may have certain challenges. These challenges are to be understood and analyzed by the data scientist. This can be understood by having a gist of software architectures and quality attributes.

Software Architecture and Quality Attributes

A cloud-based software system is developed by Software Architects. Such systems may be product or service that depends on the computing system. If you are building software, the main task includes the selection of the right programming language that is to be programmed. The purpose of the system can be questioned; hence, it needs to be considered. Developing and working with software architecture must be done by a highly skilled person. Most of the organizations have started implementing effective and reliable cloud environment using cloud computing. These cloud environments are deployed over to various servers, storage, and networking resources. This is used in abundance due to its less cost and high ROI.

The main benefit to data scientists or their teams is that they are using the big space in the cloud to explore more data and create important use cases. You can release a feature and have it tested the next second and check whether it adds value, or it is not useful to carry forward. All this immediate action is possible due to cloud computing.

Sharing Big Data in the Cloud

The role of Big Data is also vital while dealing with the cloud as it makes it easier to track and analyze insights. Once this is established, big data creates great value for users.

The traditional way was to process wired data. It became difficult for the team to share their information with this technique. The usual problems included transferring large amounts of data and collaboration of the same. This is where cloud computing started sowing its seed in the competitive world. All these problems were eliminated due to cloud computing, and gradually, teams were able to work together from different locations and overseas as well. Therefore, cloud computing is very vital in both Data Science as well as Big data. Most of the organizations make use of the cloud. To illustrate, a few companies that use the cloud are Swiggy, Uber, Airbnb, etc. They use cloud computing for sharing information and data.

Cloud and Big data Governance

Working with the cloud is a great experience as it reduces resource cost, time, and manual efforts. But the question arises that how organizations deal with security, compliance, governance? Regulation of the same is a challenge for most companies. Not limited to Big data problems, but working with the cloud also has its issues related to privacy and security. Hence, it is required to develop a strong governance policy in your cloud solutions. To ensure that your cloud solutions are reliable, robust, and governable, you must keep it as an open architecture.

Need for Data Cloud Tools to Deliver High Value of Data

Demand for a data scientist in this era is increasing rapidly. They are responsible for helping big and small organizations to develop useful information from the data or data set that is provided. Large organizations carry massive data that needs to analyze continuously. As per recent reports, almost 80% of the unstructured data received by the organizations are in the form of social media, emails, i.e., Outlook, Gmail, etc., videos, images, etc. With the rapid growth of cloud computing, data scientists deal with various new workloads that come from IoT, AI, Blockchain, Analytics, etc. Pipeline. Working with all these new workloads requires a stable, efficient, and centralized platform across all teams. With all this, there is a need for managing and recording new data as well as legacy documents. Once a data scientist is given a task, and he/she has the dataset to work on, he/she must possess the right skills to analyze the ever-increasing volumes through cloud technologies. They need to convert the data into useful insights that would be responsible for uplifting the business. The data scientist has to build an algorithm and code the program. They mostly utilize 80% of their time to gathering information, creating and modifying data, cleaning if required, and organizing data. Rest 20% is utilized for analyzing the data with effective programming. This calls for the requirement of having specific cloud tools to help the data scientist to reduce their time searching for appropriate information. Organizations should make available new cloud services and cloud tools to their respective data scientists so that they can organize massive data quickly. Therefore, cloud tools are very important for a data scientist to analyze large amounts of data at a shorter period. It will save the company's time and help build strong and robust data Models.

Conclusion

Thanks for reading till the end!

There are a lot of other coding languages out there that you are able to work with, but Python is one of the best that works for most beginner programmers, providing the power and the ease of use that you are looking for when you first get started in this kind of coding language. This guidebook took the time to explore how Python works, along with some of the different types of coding that you can do with it.

In addition to seeing a lot of examples of how you can code in Python and how you can create some of your programs in this language, we also spent some time looking at how to work with Python when it comes to the world of machine learning, artificial intelligence, and data analysis. These are topics and parts of technology that are taking off and many programmers are trying to learn more about them. And with the help of this guidebook, you will be able to handle all of these, even as a beginner in Python.

When you are ready to learn more about how to work with the Python coding language and how you can make sure that you can even use Python along with data analysis, artificial intelligence, and machine learning, make sure to check out again this guidebook to help you get started.

CPSIA information can be obtained
at www.ICGtesting.com
Printed in the USA
BVHW060729010321
601378BV00001B/227

9 781801 779630